~~Dessica~~

who is Mother
Superior in my
book, with love

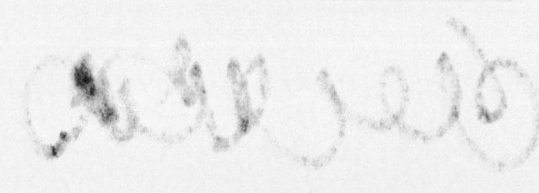

A TIME TO LAUGH

Other books by the Author:
Little Ones to Him Belong
My Id and How It Undid Me

A TIME TO LAUGH

By

WIN RICHARDSON

*A time to weep and a time to laugh...*Ecclesiastes 3:4

God made both tears and laughter and both for kind purposes. —Leigh Hunt

THE GOLDEN QUILL PRESS
Publishers
Francestown   New Hampshire

© WIN RICHARDSON 1986

Library of Congress Catalog Card Number 85-82490

ISBN 0-8233-0417-5

Printed in the United States of America

DEDICATION

*To Miss Fiditch
My ole english teach,
But for witch,
I wooden of had
the no-how to rite
this tomb. It is bound
to fill a much-needed
void.*

ACKNOWLEDGEMENTS

Some of the poems in this volume have previously appeared in the following publications: *Chrysalis, Domes and Steeples, The Shopping Bag, The Poet's Job: To Go Too Far* and *Driftwood East.*

CONTENTS

Are We a Pair?	11
To Love and Be Mute	12
The Color of Your Eyes	13
Honey-Dew, Believe Me	14
I Adore You I Think	15
Questionnaire	16
When You're Supine	17
Harmony	18
Complaint	19
Not Just Now, Muse	20
Gemini, Ascending	21
The Absolute Nadir of Nonsense	22
Fluff	23
Which Is Witch?	24
Two Could Make a Quorum	25
Quid Pro Quo	26
A Rose Is a Second Hand Rose	27
Neither	28
Have a Frog for Lunch	29
Punch Line	30
Why No Poem Today	31
Mary's Ewe	32
Rover, Move Over	33
A Bedlam of Bird Words	34
Thorb, Sittle and Bain	36
Keeping in Shape	38
The Asterisk	39

Bird Song	40
Lazy Susan	41
Victus	42
A Toast to Poetry Therapy	43
Facts and Feelings	44
Full Speed Ahead	45
Ideology	46
Quatrains	47
Generation Gap	48
Pandemonium	49
Springtime for Albert	50
Hype	51
Remedial English	52
Bafflegab Gobbledegook	54
Cant Can't Do What Candor Can	55
Cats and Dogs	56
Points of View	57
Erotic Erosion	58
A Helter Skelter Dame	59
Sauce for the Gander	60
Re-In-Car-Nation	61
Candidate for an Empty Loving Cup	62
Unisex	63
For Whom the Wedding Bells Toll	64
Different Strokes	65
Aramis Comes of Age	66
I Have Trouble With God	67
Heaven Can Wait	68
A Time to Weep	69

A TIME TO LAUGH

ARE WE A PAIR?

My love it comes ablooming
As soon as Spring arrives,
But every time I touch you
I get the hives.

I often sit and wonder
Just how my love survives,
For every time I kiss you
I get the hives.

I try to curb my passion
And check my carnal drives,
Lest something worse should happen,—and
You get the hives.

TO LOVE AND BE MUTE

I
To love and be mute
is one attribute
of a flea,
or a tree
but not me.

II
To love and be mute
is cute
in your wee
progeny,
I agree.

III
To love and be mute
is astute
to flee
first degree
bigamy.

IV
But to love and be mute
doesn't suit
ecstasy
with thee.
No, siree!

THE COLOR OF YOUR EYES

There is a shade of gray
Of which the duplicate
Cannot be found in clay
Or any roof of slate.

No autumn haze or mist
Nor smoke from burning hay
Creates an equal shade,
Your own peculiar gray.

Not cloud-infested skies
Nor habit of a nun
Precisely fits that hue,
A rare and unique one.

And since you went away
The memory I prize
Of when you said goodbye:
The color of your eyes.

HONEY-DEW, BELIEVE ME

I gave you two ripe melons,—
Indeed they were immense—
You noted their rotundity
And straightway took offense.

Now melons are a proper fruit
And you were most unfair
To penalize me for the fact
That melons don't grow square.

They have some other attributes
That surely should rank high:
Sweetness, perfume, subtleties
Unseen by human eye.

In Nature every function
Determines shape and size;
All facets of a metaphor
Should nicely harmonize.

To me the sweetness mattered most
Despite the melon's girth.
O honey, do believe me,
You're the sweetest thing on earth!

I ADORE YOU I THINK

I'm sure that you can cook,
That your pancakes are delicious;
Can you fit me to your life style?
I'd be glad to do the dishes.

Your skillful sewing charms me,
Makes me wish that we might wed;
I could stabilize the needle
While you infiltrate the thread.

Now, as for all the housework,
That necessary role,
If you would wash the windows
I'd clean the toilet bowl.

But cooking, sewing, housework
Would constitute but half;
I'd lighten up your dismal days
And try to make you laugh.

This covers all the bases
Except who'll drive the car;
That's much too complicated,—
Let's stay the way we are!

QUESTIONNAIRE

You want brown eyes
Or baby blue?
Makes no difference,
Either will do.

Dark brown hair
Or lighter hue?
Couldn't care less,
However it grew.

Six feet tall
Or five foot two?
I won't worry
About the view.

Hard to get close to
Or sticky as glue?
Stop asking questions;
I want you.

WHEN YOU'RE SUPINE

When you're supine
I'm prone to take
You out to dine
And order steak.

When you're supine
You're prone to lure;
Is that a sign
I'm insecure?

When you're supine
I'm prone to stray
Far out of line,
Or so you say.

When you're supine
So prone to lure
I'll make you mine
And keep you pure!

HARMONY

Love makes music
Wherever it is found.
You and I produce
A three note sound.

It's that third note,
If and when we meet,
Missing when you're absent,
That makes the music sweet.

COMPLAINT

It must be confessed
To marry takes courage
For I want to nest
But he wants to forage.

One love and one only
Suffices for me,
But he would be lonely
With fewer than three.

I've put my hope chest
In permanent storage,
For I want to nest
But he wants to forage.

NOT JUST NOW, MUSE

I feel your hand upon my brow;
the Muse eschews a poem just now.
Your nose is but an inch from mine,
no impulse bids me scan the line.
Your whisper slips from parted lips
seeking mine. To hell with quips!
Let others write of grief and death.
Right now I'm slightly out of breath.

GEMINI ASCENDING

He vacillates from prudence to desire,
He alternates from icicle to fire,
The everfickle tilt of Cupid's bow
Determines whether he will come or go.

She hesitates to show her secret heart
Although she'd found him handsome from the start.
At last resourceful Cupid had his say:
The twins were born a week ago today.

THE ABSOLUTE NADIR OF NONSENSE

The absolute nadir of Nonsense, I think,
Is a verse so bad it's a waste of ink,
When thoughts go astray, refusing to link
And figures of speech all die at the brink,
The sort of stuff you'd tell to a shrink,
A leaky boat about to sink.

FLUFF

Ball hit high
It's a fly.

Insect wee
It's a flea.

Ice and snow
It's a floe.

Broken jaw
It's a flaw.

Sneeze kerchoo!
It's the flu.

Silly fluff?
Sure enough.

WHICH IS WITCH?

How tell
A witch?
She zap
To have
A cat
That's black.
She zap
Besides
To zoom
Astride
A broom.

TWO COULD MAKE A QUORUM

Beetles haunt my garden
   though Science tries to aid me
with quick exterminators,
   but two, at least, evade me.

As time goes by, their progeny
   arrive a thousand strong,
from hidden nooks and crannies,
   a hardy, munching throng.

I see in this a parable
   that humans can survive
and like the beetles battle
   to keep the race alive.

If gleefully with atom bombs
   some devil should essay
to rid the world of people,
   two, too, might get away.

QUID PRO QUO

Here are some words to be discussed:
A Roman *osculum* meant you were bussed,
Basium showed an affectionate trust,
Suavium parted the lips in lust,
But I don't know the word for bust,
Nor will we list a passionate thrust.
Roman *feminae* probably fussed,
Their *homines* needed no word for rust,
"By Jove," said a Roman when he cussed,
A *ventus* was a windy gust,
Aequus meant equal as well as just,
R.I.P. These initials must
Stand for Romans turned to dust.

A ROSE IS A SECOND HAND ROSE

Digital watches have no second hand.
The reason's not too hard to understand.
Those second hands the makers never use
They give to certain folks they choose;
And one of these it's easy to infer:
Second hand Rose, no doubt you've heard of her!

NEITHER

NEITHER was the name
Of a very, very tame
    Pet beaver.
Whenever NEITHER made
Her beaver barricade
    I'd leave her.
Falling trees would thud
Then she applied the mud
    With her paw.
Working privately
No one would ever see
    NEITHER gnaw.

HAVE A FROG FOR LUNCH

"Obviously frogs are good for mankind. So next time you're in a kindly mood, have a frog to lunch, not for it." —*Saturday Review* 2/16/80 p.5

To have a frog to lunch
As prompted by this quote
Seemed like a pleasant hunch;
I found a frog of note.
"Let's dine tomorrow noon,"
I said, "and out of doors."
He answered, "Make it soon.
At my new pad or yours?"

PUNCH LINE

A mortician had a talented wife,
An accomplished singer was she;
At funerals she often rendered
"Nearer My God To Thee."

Her husband would drive the car
That carried the corpse to the grave.
Are you ready? Here comes the punch line
That nothing, no nothing, can save:

They'd been most happily married,
They'd known both better and worse,
Two towels hung in their bathroom
Were labelled HYMNS and HEARSE.

WHY NO POEM TODAY

The rhythm's wrong,
The meter's bad
Nothing's right,
It's very sad.
However hard I try to think,
The words are just a waste of ink.
My Muse, in spite of all I've tried,
Is otherwise preoccupied.
All the lines that will not scan
I've tossed into the rubbish can.
Now the can's completely full,
O why are all my thoughts so dull?
I'll put a match to where the trash is
And so consign the stuff to ashes.
Pegasus, help me! Save the day!
Alas! All he can do is neigh.

MARY'S EWE

Mary had a little ewe,
Fed it fodder mixed with glue;
Mary's proud and, sad but true,
Mary's ewe is stuck up too.

ROVER, MOVE OVER

My neighbor's dog is never mean
His sense of etiquette is keen,
He likes to keep his own yard clean,
Prefers my lawn for his latrine.

A BEDLAM OF BIRD WORDS

To stuff a tufted puffin,
With a meagre meal of muffin,
To lure or cure a skua
Or keep a kookaburra,
To woo a wary kiwi,
An apteryx or pewee,
To grab a grebe or phoebe,
Or an auk wherever he be,

To rouse a ruddy eider
Or warn a wily whydah,
To trap a tiny towhee
By some preposterous ploy,
To catch a cautious coot
And a few sea mews to boot,
To abduct a huge anhinga
To perch upon your finger,

To wake a woozy lapwing
Or hear a jaehar tapping,
To watch a lapwing limp
Or soar just like a blimp,
To have a hoopoo coo,
See an albatross or two,
To get a gaping gaylag,
Snare a spoonbill in a gray bag,

May drive you out of mind.
But all these birds you'll find,
(Some common, some not very)
In any dictionary.

THORB, SITTLE AND BAIN

When plagued by strife or stress or strain
I bend my efforts to retain
My thorb, my sittle and my bain.

When all my dreams go down the drain
I try to cling with might and main
To thorb, to sittle and to bain.

My store of joy may wax and wane,
Yet still *some* blessings *do* remain,
Some thorb, some sittle and some bain.

When worry drives me half insane,
And peace of mind is sought in vain,
There's thorb and sittle and/or bain.

I may be stranded in the rain.
So what? It's silly to complain;
Instead I thorb and sittle bain.

If some dilemma bugs my brain,
I make the choice most apt to gain
A thorb or sittle or some bain.

Cause and effect provide a chain
And though the pattern's seldom plain
Thorb may cause sittle to be bain.

Every time I miss the train
I take the next and try again
To thorb the sittle with the bain.

KEEPING IN SHAPE

A
MAN
I KNO
W LIKES
POEMS THA
T SUGGEST T
HE SHAPE OF A
T
R
E
E

A
LSO
A FEW
WANT PO
ETRY SHAP
ED LIKE
A DIA
MON
D

I THINK IDEALISM
IS IMPORTANT BUT
MOST OF MY POEMS
ARE IN THE SHAPE
OF A DOLLAR BILL

THE ASTERISK

The asterisk, it must be said,
Is not a vicious demon,
Though from its name we might be led
To think it ought to be one.

Perky, perched atop a word,
A writer's neat convention,
An asterisk may be preferred
To redirect attention.

A tiny tittle that will set
The stage for some small fact
Related to the text, and yet
Will not louse up the act.***

       ***Hi!

BIRD SONG

Certain birds are lauded
as supremely worthy species
And owe their reputation
to literary pieces.

What's so good about a dove?
Associations? Yes.
But once I had a dove that made
a most undovely mess.

An over-rated bit of rhyme
that every student meets
Is to a nameless nightingale
extolled by Mr. Keats.

The raven got a boost from Poe
as an omen non-propitious;
Its everlasting "Nevermore"
is much too repetitious.

Now only God can make a tree,
this fact I'm sure you've heard,
But with a well-turned metaphor
a poet can make a bird.

LAZY SUSAN

Round and round she spins to serve,
Lacking neither zeal nor verve;
Belies the lazy in her name,
Wish that I could do the same!

VICTUS

Invictus I'm not, nor does it appear
I'll master my fate for many a year;
So, thanks to whatever gods there be
Invictus was written by Henley, not me!
I find my soul, by fate, of late,
Reduced to a very vincible state.

A TOAST TO POETRY THERAPY

I used to shout and loudly rant
More than I realized;
Before, I could, but now I can't
Since I've been therapized.

I used to keep each secret doubt
Carefully disguised;
I've learned to write and let it out
Since I've been therapized.

I found some rigid views of mine
Needed to be revised;
An open mind is a good sign
Since I've been therapized.

Sometimes I got so paranoid
I thought I was despised,
But now such fears have been destroyed
Since I've been therapized.

Before, I used to put great store
In how I was advised,
But now I trust my inner core
Since I've been therapized.

The Muse can be your therapist,
S/he should be recognized.
You may not be a lyricist
But you'll be therapized.

FACTS AND FEELINGS

Feelings matter more than facts
Unless you are a computer;
For feelings may result in acts
Mere facts won't make you cuter.

Though feelings cause some woe
And set the brain areeling,
Here's the wisest way to go:
Combine the facts with feeling.

FULL SPEED AHEAD

They say it's a sin to relinquish
The truths that we've often been told;
That it's folly to voice opinions
Which differ too much from the old;
That it's wrong to defy conventions,-
An error ascribed to one's youth;
That it's foolish to try something novel
When scouting the hideout of Truth;
That it's unwise to disregard custom
In shaping the course of life's span;
That no good can come from ignoring
An ancient and time-tested plan.
But God, from whose infinite wisdom
Has come the strength of the few,
Forgive, if I pray for the courage
To cherish and seek something new.

IDEOLOGY

Deep within the heart is hid
A precious something Freud called id
To all desires it holds the key
Id is a causative quantity.

It calls the climber up the mountain
It is a kind of inner fountain,
A source of boundless energy,
Id is an infinite quantity.

Id is what every doctor needs,
Id is the Sister telling beads,
It can't be measured from A to Z,
Id is an unknown quantity.

Additive X makes butter better,
But id is more than a magic letter;
Like the Greek pi and Vitamin C
Id is a basic quantity.

No one is able to fully define
The various factors that must combine
To give us a lasting fidelity
But id is a noble quantity.

QUATRAINS

I
You don't tell lies to children,
The Truth, though brutal, it seems
Will far surpass deception;
It lets them retain their dreams.

II
She has a caloric diet,
And keeps it to the letter;
She knows, in female figures,
Bigger is seldom better.

III
That dog drenched in mustard mused
This observation droll:
"I sometimes get a bit confused
When I am on a roll."

IV
The skin of our teeth has a way
Of making it perfectly clear
That being foolish today
Will make us wiser next year.

V
"What is the secret of life?"
Some callow youth may ask.
"The fullest use of your talent
In some productive task."

GENERATION GAP

The gap we each must fill
Is really nothing new;
A parent's roll is still
To keep on growing too.

When elders whom they see
Are dull and flat,
The children's normal plea
Is, "God, save me from that."

In time, the part each plays
Will be reversed,
And both will find new ways
Quite strange and unrehearsed.

PANDEMONIUM

With Rock and Roll poor Pan is on
  the rack;
Never more will "moon in June"
  come back.
All melody, it seems, has been
  foresworn;
Grace notes have passed away,
  the beat goes on.
Poor Pan! When "music" rivals
  sonic boom,
Love lacks the mood it needs
  to bloom.
The ever-mounting noise from
  turned-up tape
Permits no tenderness,
  just rape.

SPRINGTIME FOR ALBERT

"Alligator in zoo persists in sterility in spite of stimulation by French horn player." —*TIME Magazine* 6/9/47

"Albert Gator, do you hear that sound?
The time is ripe to be up and around."

"Listen, Mrs. Alice Gator,
I'll say it now and prove it later:

That is a fake as sure as you're born;
I guess I can tell an old French horn.

I'm not about to come in late
If and when we plan to mate.

So tell that tooter to go away;
You're the one I want to stay.

Sterility? Nonsense! That's old hat;
In forty-seven it might have been that,

But now the times have changed, you see
And I just had a vasectomy."

HYPE

"This paper towel's phenomenal,
Absorbs whatever you wipe,
And very economical."
So goes the usual hype.

"Our tenderizer will save a
Chop that's tougher than tripe
And add delightful flavor."
So goes the usual hype.

"JUICOO is just divine,
From oranges tangy and ripe,
Sweetened by steady sunshine."
So goes the usual hype.

"To whiten dentures simply soak
Your teeth in DIPPYDIPE,
Designed for all the folks who smoke."
So goes the usual hype.

"Ladies, whenever a headache
Makes you fret or gripe,
SUPERSLOP's the thing to take."
So goes the usual hype.

By now I've had enough
Of each wearisome stereotype.
Refusing to buy the awful stuff,
I say, "To Hell with hype."

REMEDIAL ENGLISH

What you need for a sailboat
Is a brisk and lively wind;
You spell it W-I-N-D and then
It rhymes with pinned and skinned.

What you do to a watch
Has a sound of a different kind;
It's also W-I-N-D
But you pronounce it wind.

You see it's never certain
Exactly what is meant
Does C-O-N-T-E-N-T
Mean con' tent or content' ?

An accent sometimes alters
What certain words betoken;
Communication falters
Unless those words are spoken.

A novice may make booboos
However hard he tries;
Pronunciations vary,
They're hard to analyze.

With these two quirks of English
You'd think we'd have enough,

But there are three more oddities
In *through* and *cough* and *tough*.

Though similar in spelling,
Each has a different sound;
For unfamiliar aliens
The booby-traps abound.

BAFFLEGAB GOBBLEDEGOOK

The sesquipedelial words
Found in many a technical book
Resembles the twitter of birds:
Bafflegab gobbledegook.

When a teenager makes with the jive
And flaunts that superior look,
It's cool and hep, man alive!
Bafflegab gobbledegook.

When a doctor wants to prescribe
What and how much should be took,
The result is hard to describe:
Bafflegab gobbledegook.

And now we have the computer,
Which does everything but cook;
For them we'll need a tutor:
Babblegab gobbledegook.

CANT CAN'T DO WHAT CANDOR CAN

At the Rolls Royce plant in England
    It is generally agreed:
"Our cars will never break down.
    Instead they may fail to proceed."

An army never retreats
    When it's evident they are losing;
It's rather "intended withdrawal,
    A defense of our own choosing."

A man who pursues a maiden
    Will claim when he loses the race,
"I didn't really love her,
    I always enjoy a good chase."

It's always the "image" we're after,
    A spurious role that's played;
Why can't we embrace reality
    And call a spade a spade?

CATS AND DOGS

To those who have 'em and come to know 'em
   A dog is prose and a cat's a poem.
Dogs may be smelly and tend to drool
   While cats are fastidious, as a rule.
A dog, to please you, will stand on tip-toes
   But Puss looks haughtily down her nose.
When a dog gets wet he thinks it's swell
   But cats and water don't mix very well.
Dogs seldom balk at a ride in a car;
   Cats prefer walking, no matter how far.
Dogs get the mange and often have fleas
   While cats chase birds and climb up trees.
Sometimes a dog lets his dignity down,
   Wagging his tail and playing the clown.
He'll bury a juicy bone with care
   But cats sniff their food and leave it there.
If cats are black, the old wives tell
   They can generate a mystical spell.
One thing you'll learn about these two;
   You may own a dog but a cat owns you.

POINTS OF VIEW

"Nude" is poetry
    "Naked" is prose;
Which would you be
    Without your clothes?

"Naked" is naughty,
    Might cause a fuss;
But "nude" is arty,
    Accounted a plus.

"Au natural"
    Makes no one blanch;
Things are less *mal*
    Quand on dit French.

Another way
    Is "in the buff"
Shoudn't we say
    This is enough?

"In the raw"
    Will also fit;
Just one more
    Then we'll quit.

Last, when bare,
    It's equally cute
To say "I'll wear
    My birthday suit."

EROTIC EROSION

I'd rather hug than kiss
That way you get more touch,
And when it comes to bliss,
A man can't have too much.

When passion proves too weak
And I must come to grips
With a peck upon the cheek,
I'd rather kiss her lips.

When hugs and kisses fail
I quickly understand
No technique will prevail
Except to hold her hand.

When I was one and twenty,
As every young man does,
(Of lust I had a plenty)
And wanted all there was.

But now, at three score years,
I'm not about to quibble;
Less bold, and full of fears,
I'm quite content to nibble.

A HELTER SKELTER DAME

Helter skelter to the core,
She seldom knows the score;
Though her motives may be pure
She is never very sure.

Her color schemes all clash,
Her favorite dish is hash,
Her chatter never stops,
She is prone to malaprops.

Her curtains lack a valance,
Her bank account won't balance,
With a vacillating brain
She's a spinning weathervane.

But in this wavering dame
One thing only stays the same:
Superficial traits may alter
But her love will never falter.

SAUCE FOR THE GANDER

"Wordsworth's wife would have got more attention in his lines if she had been a mountain, a lake or an idiot."
—*N. Y. Times* Book Review

"Mrs. Wordsworth, when do we eat?"
Asked the hungry, poetical Will.
Quick as a mouse replied his spouse,
"Go ask yon wooded hill."

"Mrs. Wordsworth, prithee hug me,
Show you love me still."
Unsatisfied, his wife replied,
"Go pluck a daffodil."

RE-IN-CAR-NATION

If you could have a second turn
Upon this global ball,
What form would be your chief concern,
Your dearest wish of all?

A wife who heard this query
Stifled a bitter ha ha,
And said, a wee bit weary,
"I'd be my husband's car."

CANDIDATE FOR AN EMPTY LOVING CUP

She's anxious to reduce
So she'll appeal to him,
Subsists on orange juice
To keep her figure trim.

She picks her sweets with care
Lest calories run riot,
She'd sooner risk starvation
Than abrogate her diet.

For tidbit deprivation
And thirsts that she denies,
There ought to be a trophy,
A non-caloric prize.

UNISEX

We live in an age of clinical sex
as brutal as kidney transplants.
No longer are blushes sufficient index
of love once shown by a glance.
Could be that the amorous gyre
pirouettes in the same old dance,
but it's not so easy to tell by attire
when they both are wearing the pants.

FOR WHOM THE WEDDING BELLS TOLL

You lads who go acourting
Might just as well quit;
Since women make the choices
That's the truth of it.

If perchance she should decide
To put you to the test,
Accept your fate with cheerfulness
And hope it's for the best.

One thing is known for certain:
Though great the suitor's skill,
No man can win a woman's heart
Against her will.

DIFFERENT STROKES

If love is rational (which I doubt)
The reasons may turn inside out.
Irrational love, a sturdier thing,
Survives whatever time may bring.

Sex is cheap, affection's dear,
You have to keep the difference clear.
So closely are the two entwined
They thwart the efforts of the mind.

Men tend to leave their love to chance,
Their fantasies they treasure,
Evaluate each new romance
By just the present pleasure.

Women want their love to last,
Good for many a mile,
Constant, once the die is cast,
They love a long, long while.

ARAMIS COMES OF AGE

i.

Our tiny kitten, Aramis,
Bites the hand he means to kiss.
Untaught, he lacks the loving touch
That shows he loves us very much.

ii.

Likewise young men may lack finesse
And overlook the sweet caress,
Engaging in a feckless search,
They leave their partner in the lurch.

iii.

Some day our Aramis will learn
A better way he should return
Affection. He will then confer
A cuddly snuggle and a purr.

iv.

So older men, their rashness spent,
Will make their loved ones more content,
Perhaps by waxing sentimental
And tactics much more warm and gentle.

I HAVE TROUBLE WITH GOD

I have trouble with God,
    An enigma, He
Moves in a mist
    Of mystery.

At times I say
    In perplexity,
What in Hell
    Is He doing to me?

How can I love Him,
    My prayers denied,
I often fear
    He's not on my side.

The world is rife
    With untold pain,
I plan a parade
    And He sends rain.

I have trouble with God,
    But this I'll say:
Amid the darkness
    I'm *toujours gai*.

I have trouble with God,
    Oh why can't I see
The fault is my own;
    He has trouble with me!

HEAVEN CAN WAIT

Alas! I've never learned a thing
On how celestial choirs sing.

I'm sure I'd be an awful flop
At tuning up an angel's harp.

Had I to catch a falling star
I doubt if I could run that far.

How do you dust a fleecy cloud?
Are bamboo-handled brooms allowed?

It's not my dish to wear a crown
So push that button labeled DOWN.

Hold that hell-bound elevator.
Bye! St. Peter! See you later.

A TIME TO WEEP

"But a certain maid beheld him...by the fire."
—Luke XXII:56

It was Peter the maid beheld
   sitting by the fire.
She, thinking to recognize him, said,
   "Good sir, may I inquire

Is not this man your Master, —
   The one they've led away?"
But Peter scowled in silence
   and finally answered, "Nay."

A second time she asked him,
   Again he answered no;
His loyalty had faltered,
   His love was burning low.

Came once again the query:
   "Have I been so misled?
Methinks he counted you his friend."
   But Peter hung his head.

"I've never seen the man before."
   And ere the phrase was done
A cock crowed thrice. The morning light
   announced the rising sun.

Just so the darkness vanished
    from Peter's troubled mind,
His Master's words came back to him
    in prophecy designed.

"Before the cock shall crow three times..."
    too late poor Peter knew
he had, alas, denied his Lord;
    His heart was filled with rue.

While Peter wept most bitterly,
    Christ went his way alone
That Life might triumph over Death
    and God's love might be shown.

When Peter met his Lord again
    there was no cause to weep;
The Master only smiled and said,
    "Now, Peter, feed my sheep."